Lorin Blodget

The Commercial And Financial Strength of the United States

Lorin Blodget

The Commercial And Financial Strength of the United States

ISBN/EAN: 9783744708463

Printed in Europe, USA, Canada, Australia, Japan

Cover: Foto ©ninafisch / pixelio.de

More available books at **www.hansebooks.com**

COMMERCIAL AND FINANCIAL STRENGTH

OF THE

UNITED STATES.

THE

COMMERCIAL AND FINANCIAL

Strength of the United States,

AS SHOWN IN

THE BALANCES OF FOREIGN TRADE

AND THE

INCREASED PRODUCTION OF STAPLE ARTICLES.

BY LORIN BLODGET.

PHILADELPHIA:
KING & BAIRD, PRINTERS, No. 607 SANSOM STREET.
1864.

The only just and adequate measure of the national resources, is to be reached through a calculation of the quantities of all articles of value produced, and of the exchanges, both of quantities and values, conducted with foreign countries. An exaggerated scale of prices laid on articles of production, does not constitute wealth absolutely, though full prices are always favorable, and if a balance of exchanges with foreign nations exists in our favor, high prices bring us more, and constitute a decided national advantage. Nor does an abundance of staple articles produced constitute wealth, if the exchanges with other countries exhaust us through the payment of heavy annual balances. The two vital points of inquiry in a case of national trial are therefore these we have named, and they are directly connected in their practical consequences. It is proposed to offer some statement of facts illustrating them which have not been given to the public heretofore. The minds of all patriotic and earnest men are now struggling to solve the question, whether the resources of the United States are adequate to the present emergency, and whether we can or cannot furnish the vast sums necessary to meet the great trial the rebellion has brought on the country.

The writer claims that the resources of the country in articles of material and actual wealth are far greater than the generally accepted estimate makes them; that the quantities of these great staple articles are greater in a degree even beyond the increase of prices, and that all forms of production,

*
(5)

from the crudest agricultural or mineral staples, to the highest fabrics of manufacturing skill, have advanced on an average one-half in 1863, over the production of 1860. This is the sharpest contrast which can be suggested, 1860 being far the most productive year before the war, and 1863 being the year of severest trial caused by the war. If the resources of the country were, or are now short or inadequate on any point this comparison cannot fail to develop the truth of the case, and if they are ample and the country is strong in consequence, this also cannot fail to appear.

In view of the results disclosed in the following statements, it is not easy to refrain from expressing surprise at the opinions generally prevalent. The facts are in most cases well-known to the public, but they have been neutralized by counter-statements, deceptive statistics and by mere declamation to such a degree that they are almost reversed in their significance. The practical action of intelligent citizens is generally nearly correct; business is prosecuted with energy, and the loans offered by the government are taken with unprecedented freedom and confidence. But the statements and opinions expressed by what are usually recognized as commercial and financial authorities are widely and grossly in error. They constantly assert, and appear to prove, that to be impossible which is daily done triumphantly in spite of these adverse prophecies. The inference derived from these professed authorities would be fairly expressed in placing our productive resources at one-half less in 1863, than they were in 1860, whereas they are proved by indisputable statistics to be one-half greater.

In regard to foreign exchanges, there is especially injurious misapprehension. Contrary to the impression almost universally prevalent, foreign exchanges do not draw an exhausting balance from us, nor have they done so in recent years, at least not since 1858. Still more important is the fact that since the war the balances in favor of the United States in foreign trade have increased greatly over those of any year immediately preceding. This balance was twice as great in 1862–3 as it was in 1859–60, being in the last named year $37,958,000, while in 1862–3 it was $79,631,000. This single fact is significant of the extent of the misapprehension which false or imperfect statistics have produced. It is undoubtedly the prevalent belief that for the last three years particularly, the course of foreign trade has been heavily against us.

In the following statements it may appear that the natural order of arrangement is inverted, and that the detail of resources should have been given first in order. But the chief point of interest is really the conclusion or final result, as expressed in the totals of trade compared. The explanation or citation of supporting facts is the second point examined, and it is, therefore, left in that order. The statements of actual production given in that place furnish a body of evidence that cannot be impeached, though they are necessarily limited to certain classes of productions, and mainly to those which are transported and exported nearly crude as agricultural or mineral staples. Manufactured articles cannot be readily identified, and their values or quantities put in statistical form, and though they evidently fully sustain the course of increase observed in other classes, we are compelled to pass them over here, and to rely mainly on the proved wealth of the country in comparatively crude products. Every one who observes carefully the activity of manufacturing production is aware that this department fully keeps pace with the progress of trade in exportable staples. The products of skilled labor in the United States were never so abundant, never so largely exported, or so freely called for in the local markets of consumption.

EXCHANGES AND BALANCES IN FOREIGN TRADE.

There is very general solicitude to obtain clear and definite information as to the state of the commercial exchanges of the United States with foreign countries, and as to the financial consequences resulting from these exchanges. Many persons have probably been incredulous as to the constantly repeated assertions that the balance of trade was ruinously against us, but it has not been easy to verify or disprove the statements. The materials at command for the purpose of forming a judgment have been insufficient. The current published values of trade at New York are by no means full representatives of the entire trade of the country, nor are these either fairly stated or fairly construed, in most cases, in the original channels of publication. The statistical volumes finally put forth by the government are late in appearing, and are rarely quoted from in financial articles. The result is a prevalent belief that our foreign commerce has exhausted the country, and drained us of gold to a ruinous degree. At the same time there are evidences of an under current of disbelief in these asserted calamities, even on the part of those who constantly repeat them. The present unprecedented prosperity in every department of the industry and business of the country is declared by theorists to be fallacious, and certain to result in contraction and collapse, yet this is practically doubted by most of those concerned in business, and by most of those whose support of the government, and whose confidence in its financial soundness, is really necessary.

Certainly the evidence should be most conclusive, which would warrant the public or the Government in accepting the present factitious and absurd price of gold as a measure of the depreciation of the currency, or of the decline of real values in the United States. An annual balance of trade against the country of seventy-five to one-hundred millions yearly, could nɔt in five years produce consequences warranting such relative prices. No other cause or process of exhaustion exists. No reason exists for reducing the dollar to half its usual value, or for rating lands, houses, and other property at a value not above half that they bore in 1860. Yet either this conclusion must be accepted, or the assumption that the price of gold is now the measure of all values must be rejected. The fact is that in foreign trade there is no balance against the country, and there has been none for years. On the contrary, for six years past the balance of exchanges with all foreign countries has been uniformly in favor of the United States, and this by steadily increasing sums. It has been larger since the war began than before, and it was larger in 1863 than in any year since the foundation of the Government, reaching nearly the sum of eighty millions of dollars.

The writer is aware that many persons will express decided incredulity at this statement, but the corrected official statistics of the British government, as well as those of the United States, which here follow, are conclusive against all cavil. They substantially agree also, except in the higher sum which the British tables give as the balance in our favor—an average difference of ten or twelve millions of dollars yearly.

It must not be forgotten that a powerful commercial interest has done its utmost, from the commencement of the present troubles, to embarrass the Government, and to mislead both the authorities and the people as to the extent of the National resources. For this purpose it was always easy to put forth partial figures, and to place a false construction on so much as was published. It is but the simple truth to say that this use of commercial figures has been the invariable rule with a large number of publications usually taken as commercial authorities, and generally received and quoted through the country. When the relative values of exports and imports too plainly disproved the asserted exhaustion, it became the rule to state in advance that the exports were in depreciated values, and that their sum must be reduced by one-half, or in some other proportion, to correspond with the gold values of the imports. There are two or three decisive reasons that no such reduction is necessary. In the first place, exchange was below par two to five per cent. during almost the entire year 1861, and if gold is held to follow, as well as to control, exchange, it might reasonably be held that gold was also below par. Nor did either gold or exchange rise to any noticeable premium until June, 1862, and therefore no reduction can be claimed as applicable to any year or period of those here compared, except the last, the fiscal year 1862-3. The British official statement of exports and imports brought down to the beginning of 1864, show that the same relative values in their currency continued for every month to the close of 1863, at least; and that the balance in our favor was even larger, by several millions, than our own figures made it. As a rule also, exports from all counties are undervalued, and particularly from the United States they have been both undervalued, and have gone out without being fully reported. The deficiency on this last account amounts to several millions yearly. Again, exporters in 1862 and 1863, when immense shipments of produce were made for the primary purpose of creating exchange to sell, hold, or speculate in, to a great extent reported their cargoes at the custom-house in exchange values, not altered to correspond with any supposed depreciation of the currency.

In 1861 and 1862 the hue and cry raised against the financial strength of the United States induced the return of many millions of United States securities, held abroad, for sale or reimbursement in our markets. There were not less than fifty millions of these in value, and perhaps ten millions more might be assumed, yet they were taken with the utmost ease, and paid for in the natural surplus produce of the country. And not only was this done, but the United States drew from Europe in one year forty millions of gold in addition—by the British account $35,728,652 in the calendar year 1861, and by the United States account $46,339,611 in the fiscal year 1860–61, and $16,415,000 in 1861-2—an overwhelming and unanswerable proof of the commercial strength of the country. It is surprising that this remarkable course of events, continued as it was near to the middle of 1862, has received so little notice by financial writers. Since that time there has been no marked reversal of the ordinary course of things in foreign trade. We have exported the natural surplus of gold as we did before the war, and apart from the insanity ruling the gold market, trade is perfectly easy and quiet.

It has been the official duty of the writer of this paper to collate the records of the United States relating to foreign commerce, and to prepare them for publication in the usual channels, the finance report, and the reports on commerce and navigation. Whatever conditions of reporting or preparation may be calculated to modify the external values of any such statement thus become fully known, and a corrected final result may be attained. Thus the commercial exchanges of the fiscal year ending June 30, 1861, were first made public only to the extent that actual returns were made to the Treasury Department, no estimate being then made to cover the deficient return of commerce for ports which lapsed into rebellion soon after. Trade continued at Charleston, Savannah, Mobile, and New Orleans, down to near the close of the fiscal year, but no returns of such trade were transmitted to the Treasury Department from any port but Charleston, after September, 1860. The chief part of the cotton crop of 1860 went out while the ports were yet open, yet very little of it did so previous to the close of September, and none of it was therefore actually embraced in the published report of trade for 1860-61. It was proposed by the writer, in October, 1863, to estimate for this omitted export, which was known to be unusually large—really much larger than in any previous year, as the British record of receipts of cotton from the United States shows—and to take as such estimate the quantities and values of corresponding periods of the previous fiscal year. The time taken was only such as corresponds with the actual continuance of commerce at each port. By direction of the Secretary of the Treasury the correction was made on these principles, and the result was embodied in the tables of the Finance Report for 1863. The uncorrected tables gave a total of exports of $249,344,913, and of imports of $335,650,153, an apparent balance against the

United States of $86,305,240. But correcting the exports by restoring the unreported values, the totals become

Exports,	$410,856,818
Imports,	352,075,535
Balance in favor of U. S.	$58,881,283

This sum is no doubt less than the real balance, since the proceeds of almost the entire cotton crop really came to northern hands. Twenty-five millions in value of the cotton actually received in England and other parts of Europe in June, July, and August, 1861, are not here taken into account at all.

From all accessible European records the conclusion is confirmed that this correction is below the actual value of the exports of produce from Southern ports during the period unreported. As evidence of this, the British statement of cotton received from the United States is as follows, compared with the return of cotton exported to England, as stated in so much of the record as was published; the period being the year ending June 30, 1861:

	Pounds.	Value.
British receipts of cotton,	968,006,928	$140,961,448
U. S. report of exports of cotton,	207,342,265	22,651,923
Cotton not accounted for,	760,664,663	$118,309,525

It will be observed that the British valuation is fourteen and a half cents per pound, while the United States valuation is but eleven cents; consequently the value, one hundred and eighteen millions, is somewhat excessive in proportion to the quantity. Yet the length of time cotton is usually at sea would make the actual receipts of cotton in England, during the first half of July, at least, the exports at United States ports previous to the close of June. In July the British receipts of cotton were, in fact, enormous, being 94,087,168 pounds, valued at $15,890,930. This being the account to England only, and exclusive of the heavy shipments of cotton then made to various Continental States of Europe, it is clear that the total

**

estimated correction taken above, of $161,011,905, is too small rather than too large.

The French statement of cotton received from the United States in this period of our defective export records, is equally decisive proof that the correction here made is fully warranted. The quantity set down in our records as having been exported to France, in the fiscal year ending June 30, 1861, is 57,270,315 pounds, valued at $6,499,601; while the French official account for the year 1861, states their receipts at 241,977,527 pounds, valued at $47,323,282. As the quantity reaching France in the last part of 1861, certainly did not exceed the usual quantity for that part of the year, and was probably much less, this calendar year in their account will fairly represent our fiscal year, and it may be taken without correcting it to the precise conformity of time, as was done in the case of cotton received in England. The excess of cotton thus shown to have gone to France is, there-fore, 184,707,280 pounds, valued there at $40,823,681. These very large quanties are conclusive evidence that it would be reasonable to add twenty-five millions to the general total of unrecorded exports on account of cotton sent to France at that time.

With this single general correction thus made, the comparison of the totals of foreign trade for a series of years to 1863, is as follows:

	Total Exports.	Total Imports.	Excess of Exports.
1854–5	$275,156,846	$261,468,520	$13,688,326
1855–6	326,964,908	314,639,942	12,324,966
1856–7	362,960,682	360,890,141	2,070,541
1857–8	324,644,421	282,613,150	42,031,271
1858–9	356,789,462	338,768,130	18,021,332
1859–60	400,122,296	362,163,941	37,958,355
1860–61	410,856,818	352,075,535	58,881,283
1861–2	229,790,280	205,819,823	23,970,457
1862–3	331,809,459	252,187,587	79,621,872

Thus the scale of excess of exports established in 1854–5, rises gradually and steadily to 1863. Its average for the last two years, the worst of the war, is $51,800,000 each year. Its average for the two years preceding the war, 1858-9 and 1859-60, was $28,000,000 each year only. For the last period of six years the total excess of exports is $260,484,570, an annual average of $43,414,095 ; and for the last three years an annual average of $54,161,204.

This is the simple face of the commercial statement. It includes, of course, the mutual exchanges of gold, and it does not include that exchange of values technically known as exchange remittances. This last account is large ; it covers the interest and dividends payable abroad, on whatever account they may be held, whether railroad stocks and bonds, or State, municipal, and United States securities. It also cannot cover the transmission here for sale of any such securities, and the remittance of exchange drawn against produce shipments in payment for them; which is, so far as the foreign creditor is concerned, the final payment of the debt.

First we will notice the gold exchanges, in order to afford any one holding views that gold is not merchandise, the opportunity of making the previous account to correspond with his views. But it may here be said that gold is certainly merchandise in California, otherwise the exhaustion of that State would be excessive by the export of fifty to sixty millions of gold annually for fifteen years. From California, at least, gold goes to Europe as merchandise, the natural product of its soil, and the natural surplus of its general production.

The exchange of gold, or rather of coin in all forms, with all foreign countries has been as follows :

	Imports.	Exports	Excess of Exports.
1854-5	$3,659,812	$56,247,343	$52,587,531
1855-6	4,207,632	45,745,485	41,537,853
1856-7	12,461,799	69,136,922	56,675,123
1857-8	19,274,496	52,633,147	33,358,651
1858-9	6,369,703	63,887,411	57,517,708
1859-60	8,550,135	66,546,239	57,996,104
1860-61	46,339,611	29,791,080	(Excess of Imports. 16,548,531)
1861-2	16,415,052	36,886,956	20,471,904
1862-3	9,555,648	64,156,610	54,600,962

In comparison with all former years, this series constitutes a new order of things, gold going out, in greater part, not as commercial balances, but really as an exportation of the surplus of the California mines. In 1843 the excess of specie imported was $20,869,768, yet that was deemed a very unfortunate year in the general business of the country.

In 1847 there was an excess of specie imported of $22,214,265 while at the same time the balance of trade, specie included, was about $12,000,000 in our favor. Remembering the state of business generally during most of the period from 1829 to the time the gold began to be produced in California, it cannot with any reason be supposed that the prosperity of the last ten years has been a fiction, and that these sums of gold going out have caused the ruin, or at least have proved that we were ruined. It is simply the movement of a natural excess from the production of the mines, and its annual average for the last six years has been but $34,566,133. Yet this strong and natural flow of gold has been once very thoroughly reversed since the war began. In two years, beginning with July 1, 1860, and ending June 30, 1862, the total importation of gold was $62,754,662, or $31,377,331 each year. The excess of importation in 1860-61 was $15,548,501; nearly all of which came in after the war began. This remarkable period of gold importation has been observed less than it deserves to be. It really marked the great accumulated wealth of the country when few believed that such wealth existed. It proved that the Government could obtain its loans from its own people, although this possibility was decisively and constantly denied by the usual commercial authorities. The incomplete statement of exports for the fiscal year 1860-61 gave color to the belief among statisticians that the national resources were really at a low ebb, and the utmost was made of this appearance by the enemies of the finance policy of the Government.

It has been seen that the annual balance of aggregate foreign trade in favor of the United States for six years to July 1, 1863 was $43,414,095, and that the annual excess of gold sent abroad, over that imported for the same period, was only

$34,566,133. There was, therefore, a balance exclusive of gold in favor of the United States averaging annually $8,847,962. Applying this calculation to particular years it exhibits the following results: 1860–61 having a remarkably large credit account, and in fact, showing the mistake of taking gold exchanges from the calculation in any case.

Balance of foreign trade exclusive of gold:

	Against the U. S.	In favor of the U. S.
1857–8		$8,672,620
1858–9	$39,496,376	
1859–60	20,037,749	
1860–61		75,429,814
1861–62		3,498,553
1862–63		25,020,910
	$59,534,125	$112,621,897

Balance in favor of United States, $53,087,772
Or, as before stated, an annual average of $8,847,962

Taking the last three years exclusive of gold, the sum is $104,949,277 and the average $34,983,092. The excess of twenty-five millions exclusive of gold in 1862–3 is, perhaps, the most remarkable single fact that appears in this statement, since in that year there was no cotton, rice, or sugar to export, and the full effect of the war was felt in every department of trade.

The relative terms of the statements of export and import values have been alluded to, but the constant claims made that the values reported should be greatly altered because one is in depreciated currency and the other in gold, perhaps will justify further explanation. Generally the New York commercial publications claim that all export values should be changed to gold equivalents, at whatever price gold may bear at the time, before they are compared with the values of the imports. The whole claim is radically unsound because the price of gold is purely speculative and factitious. It does not represent any real relation held either by the property or the currency of the country, to property and currency in Europe.

The assumed correction to gold prices also, does not apply to the statistics here given, for reasons previously cited. The premium on gold did not exist at all until near May, 1862, and it had no commercial importance in foreign trade before the close of the fiscal year 1861-2. An advance of eight per cent. in foreign exchange was attained very near the close of the year, or after the middle of June, the fiscal year ending with that month. Up to this time. the premium on gold and exchange had not been equal, in its aggregate effect, to the reverse premium, and the depression of exchange which continued through the greater part of the year 1861. If a correction be insisted on, therefore, it applies only to the fiscal year 1862-3, the last of the series, and to the passing year 1863-4. The principal basis of the claim here made is not affected by whatever views may be held in regard to gold. The commerce of the country has demonstrated its financial soundness, and has shown that its exchanges with foreign countries are on a firmer and stronger basis than at any period of its previous history. No European nation has such resources for export, and none can command a balance in its favor so certainly as the United States.

And for plain commercial reasons it is true, and is so held in the statistics of all countries, that export commerce not paying duty is always returned short. In many countries estimated corrections are made for this short return, particularly in England and Canada.* In the United States no duties have been paid on exports, and no rigid cognizance of them has been taken, the rendering of invoices being, indeed, more formal than accurate, and for many years open to exception on the ground of want of fulness both in quantities and values. Officers of the New York customs best informed on the point estimate this under-valuation at nearer twenty per cent. than any other pro-

---

* Estimates of Canadian exports "short returned at Inland Ports."

1861,	.	.	.	.	.	$1,896,947
1862,	.	.	.	.	.	1,917,080
1863.	.	.	.	.	.	2,486,642

Trade and Navigation Report of Canada for 1863.

portion, including many exports which are by accident, oftener than by design, not on the recorded manifest at all. Clearance is granted, by the terms of our law, on the simple oath of shipper or agent, and the necessities of trade are often such that a ship cleared at midday must load much of its cargo actually after clearance, the cargo being changed entirely sometimes, and in other cases much modified from the first purpose of the parties interested. A minimum of values is always reported, for many reasons, in ordinary commercial periods. And during the war, with the temptations to blockade running, the shipments in one way or another getting out are in actual value fully twenty per cent. above the reported values.

Again, the shipments of produce for two or more years past have been largely made with the especial purpose of creating exchange, and it is said by the reporting officers that such exports are valued in the terms of the face of the exchange they create. No requirement of law touches this precise point, and it may be assumed by exporters that these are the true values required to be attested in their invoices. Thus a shipment creating exchange to the value of £10,000 sterling on Liver-pool or London is reported at $48,400, its gold value, and not its currency value.

The assumption of discrepant values is further discredited by the statements of trade made by foreign nations themselves, the British in particular. The official trade statements annually published by the British government, are very full and of most undoubted general accuracy. Both exports and imports are there rigidly scrutinized and valued, the errors of the invoices in either direction being carefully corrected. Exports from England are subjected to an official inspection not less thorough than that given in the United States to imports, while exports of the United States, as we have before shown, are subject to great errors of omission as well as of undervaluation. Although American trade to England is by no means the entire volume of foreign trade, that channel has recently absorbed a very large share of the direct trade formerly con-ducted to tropical countries of both hemispheres, and also a very large share of the trade of the United States with Continental Europe. Trade with France has relatively declined as regards direct exchanges, and no other countries or ports than those of North Germany, Hamburg, and Bremen, maintain a large and increasing direct trade with the United States. England is really the full example of all foreign trade, as well as the country to which all exchanges go in adjusting balances with nearly all countries. The following are the values exchanged between the United States and the United Kingdom of Great Britain and Ireland, as stated in the British annual reports.

British Official Statement of Trade with the United States.

	Imports from the United States.	Exports to the United States.		
		British.	Foreign and Colonial.	Total.
1856	£36,047,773	£21,918,105	£698,772	£22,616,877
1857	33,647,227	18,985,939	1,090,956	20,076,895
1858	34,257,515	14,491,448	1,302,253	15,793,701
1859	34,294,083	22,553,405	1,864,487	24,417,892
1860	44,727,202	21,667,065	1,240,616	22,907,681
1861	49,389,602	9,064,504	1,961,179	11,025,683
1862	27,715,157	14,327,870	4,846,037	19,173,907
1863		15,351,626		

Balance in favor of the United States,

1856	£13,430,896	or in U. S. values,		$65,005,536
1857	13,570,332	"	"	65,680,406
1858	18,463,814	"	"	89,364,859
1859	9,876,191	"	"	47,800,764
1860	21,819,521	"	"	105,606,481
1861	38,263,919	"	"	181,197,368
1862	8,541,250	"	"	41,339,650

This is the statement of merchandise exclusive of gold, and it gives extreme values as the difference between the two countries in favor of the United States. The following is the British official statement of gold and silver exchanged :

	Imported from U. S.	Exported to U. S.
1856	not given.	£96,227
1857	not given.	857,110
1858	£4,811,772	202,567
1859	9,672,981	14,342
1860	4,792,582	1,727,220
1861	66,683	7,381,953
1862	10,064,162	37,528
1863	8,147,524	54,195

or, in United States values,

	Imported from U. S.	Exported to U. S.	Excess to England.	Excess to U. S.
1858	$23,288,977	$980,424	$22,308,553	
1859	46,817,228	68,415	46,748,813	
1860	23,196,097	8,359,744	14,836,352	
1861	322,745	35,728,652		35,405,797
1862	48,710,544	169,535	48,541,009	
1863	39,434,016	262,303	39,171,713	

Average annual excess to England—
For three years before the war, . $27,964,573
For three years of the war, . . 17,435,642
For the entire six years, . . . 22,700,106

In whatever light this exchange of gold and silver is regarded, the state of trade is still favorable to the United States. If counted as merchandise, it increases the balance in our favor for every year except 1861. In fact the natural movement of gold is toward England as the central point of the world's exchanges, and going from the United States it is legitimate merchandise; but in going from England it is such in far less degree, and might, in fact, then be regarded as a payment of differences such as we pay in exchange now, and paid in gold before we were producers of gold. From England it is an exhausting drain, while from the United States it is not, because the United States produce vast quantities of gold. *

In the face of these enormous annual differences between the values sent to England from the United States, and those sent to the United States from England, it is not easy to see how danger can be apprehended, or why great fear should be expressed of commercial exhaustion. Any assumption that past debts exist there, the discharge of which requires the shipment of all our gold and all our surplus wealth is utterly unfounded. Trade nominally to and from England is undoubtedly largely of the character of transit trade through British ports to other markets, but the adjustment of balances is in England, and the statistics here given represents the aggregate of general commerce with a reasonable approximation to accuracy.

The United States official returns of trade with England present a list of annual balances similar to those derived from the British official statements. The values exchanged for eight fiscal years, to June 30, 1863, are as follows:

	Exports to England.	Imports from England.	Balances. Excess of Exports.
1856	$162,360,807	$122,266,082	$40,094,725
1857	185,845,784	130,803,093	55,042,691
1858	168,095,848	95,720,658	72,375,190
1859	174,945,853	125,754,421	49,191,432
1860	202,340,921	138,596,484	63,744,437
1861	228,935,894	149,206,267	79,729,527
1862	110,598,156	86,481,430	24,116,726
1863	179,776,517	113,135,700	66,640,817

If it be required to separate the gold exchanged from these totals, the following are the values of gold:

	Exports to England.	Imports from England.	Excess of Exports.
1856	$34,161,062	$421,771	$33,739,291
1857	50,890,268	4,069,054	46,721,214
1858	38,636,001	6,753,631	31,882,370
1859	33,380,575	101,371	33,279,204
1860	41,761,051	147,383	41,613,668
1861	12,164,810	34,288,466	(Excess of Imports.) (22,123,656)
1862	24,729,001	11,731,720	12,997,271
1863	51,339,267	258,499	51,070,068

Deducting the values of gold and silver exchanged from both exports and imports, and the balances become,

	In Favor of U. S.	Against U. S.
1856	6,355,434	
1857	8,321,477	
1858	40,492,820	
1859	15,912,228	
1860	22,130,709	•
1861	101,853,183	
1862	11,119,445	
1863	15,570,049	

The average in favor of the United States for three years before the war is $26,178,606; for three years of war $42,847,559, and for six years $34,513,082. But the true averages are of the totals including gold, which are,

For three years before the war,	.	$61,770,353
For three years of war,	. . .	53,495,690
For six years,	. . . . .	50,299,685

The statistics of France which give the actual values exchanged, are accessible for only three calendar years, 1859, 1860 and 1861. The total trade is stated in those reports at the following "actual values," as distinguished from a scale of "official values," quite unsuitable for comparison :

	Imports into France from the United States. Francs.	Exports from France to the United States. Francs.
1859	219,811,695	427,516,561
1860	262,778,940	364,902,478
1861	392,978,966	112,568,847

The balances therefore are,

	In favor of the United States. Francs. Dollars.	Against the United States. Francs. Dollars.
In 1859	. . . .	207,704,866 or 40,710,153
" 1860	. . . .	102,123,538 or 20,006,212
" 1861	280,410,119, or 54,960,383	•

The balance in favor of the United States in 1861 is nearly equal to the sum of the two previous years on the other side.

Our own records confirm the indications here given that the course of trade with France, changed remarkably in our favor after 1860.

	Exports to France.	Imports from France.	Excess of Exports.
1858-9	$44,299,618	$41,301,147	$ 2,998,471
1859-60	62,206,278	43,219,549	18,986,729
1860-61	60,519,334	34,245,549	26,273,783
1861-62	20,568,495	7,835,466	12,733,929
1862-63	16,530,726	10,591,624	5,939,102

Adding to the exports of 1860-61, the large amount of cotton and other southern produce known to have been received in France, the value of which, in cotton alone, is, as has been stated, probably not less than $25,000,000, and the condition of trade with that country appear very strongly in our favor, from 1860 forward.

THE INCREASED QUANTITIES OF IMPORTANT ARTICLES PRODUCED IN THE UNITED STATES.

It is not surprising that the vast expenditures caused by the war, and the heavy taxation levied in various forms to meet this expenditure, should raise grave questions of doubt in the minds of even the most patriotic men, as to the ability of the country to sustain these burdens. We are required to deal with sums unprecedently large—large almost beyond any historic parallel—and to provide for armies greater than any European State ever put in the field. The first aspect of the case is almost certain to suggest views such as were expressed by Mr. Cobden a year or more since, to the effect that this immense diversion of human energies from productive labor to the destructive occupation of war, must necessarily produce calamity and distress in the social system of the North, whether such results are immediately felt, or be for a time delayed until a temporary and deceptive prosperity, caused by the unnatural stimulus of the war, shall have run its course. These are the opinions of a friend of the United States, not of an enemy. They are very natural, and were the circumstances which surround us, as a nation, similar to those controlling almost every other nation of the world, and those of Europe in particular, the result Mr. Cobden predicts would be almost certain to follow.

But we claim here, and propose to offer abundant facts to prove the assertion, that the conditions surrounding and controlling the material prosperity of the United States are wholly unlike those existing in any similar national trial known to history: that its productive energies have not been seriously obstructed by the war on any points, while on many they have been greatly stimulated, and have attained to results of the most extraordinary character. We were far more rich in accumulated resources when the war began than our own citizens believed. Our business capital was greater, and its investment was in such form as to be almost everywhere more productive after the war began than before. There was more of material wealth at hand in the form of simple elements— more wheat, corn, meats, lumber, wool, iron, copper and gold;— each and all the crude produce of the labor and capital of the Loyal States, than existed or was produced in these States before the war. The lakes, the railroads and canals carried more of all these products to market in 1862 and 1863 than they ever carried before. And of manufactured goods and general merchandise, they also carried more in tons weight than ever before, and by large differences. The first measure of these facts we prefer to take in quantities, so that no caviler can charge the increased values to an increase of prices, or assert that an inflation of the currency has created a deceptive prosperity through fictitious values.

Nor do we see any evidence that the present prosperity, which none can deny exists in a degree far beyond anything known in a long series of years, is likely to be followed by collapse and financial ruin. Business is in most cases brought entirely clear of the former universal system of long credits, and reduced to a cash basis. In trade, whatever is done at once pays its profits and releases all parties from risk. There is no chain of mutually dependent credits through which one man's failure may put in jeopardy a dozen other men. A crash cannot come, therefore, without an extreme change in real values, yet what reasonable man can look forward to a fall in the absolute values of goods or property so great as to involve the country in financial distress? One cause only is adequate to produce such an effect: it can only occur through the defeat of the armies of the Union and the triumph of the rebellion, a contingency which no man seriously believes is possible.

The statistics of the country everywhere abound in proofs of the vast increase in the quantities of all Northern products in recent years, and particularly in the increase attained in 1863 over 1860. These years compare the best year of peace with the worst year of war, in a certain sense. In some lines of production it might have been claimed that the stimulus given by the war would be apparent in 1862 over 1861; but in 1863 the country had settled to regular pursuits, and the general result of the war must necessarily appear in the aggregate of quantities then produced. The most direct and ready measure of quantities produced in the Loyal States is probably to be found in the eastward tonnage of the chief lines of transportation. All that they carry in that direction is the produce of the country, destined to some market distant from the place of its origin, and therefore a surplus of that locality.

The following is the eastward tonnage of all classes of merchandise, (coal on the Pennsylvania road excepted,) for five years, 1859 to 1863:

Tons carried Eastward in the years

	1859.	1860.	1861.	1862.	1863.
N. Y. Canals,	2,121,672	2,854,877	2,980,144	3,402,709	3,500,000
N. Y. Central road,	570,927	730,258	881,028	1,064,128	1,044,259
Erie Railway,	550,000	725,000	827,808	974,832	1,088,110
" at Dunkirk,	153,623	229.703	317,407	364,366	326,178
Pennsylvania road,	370,763	424 579	491,334	641,433	658,055
	3,613,362	4,734,714	5,180,314	6,083,102	6,290,424

In two cases above, the exact quantities are not attainable— the canal movement of 1863, and the Erie Railway tonnage of 1859 and 1860; but as the total tonnage movement, East and West, was at hand, the proportions were calculated from the nearest year in which the distinction was given. But as the total tonnage movement is equally significant as a proof of the great increase in quantities, the following aggregates are given for these four lines:

Total Tonnage of Merchandise moved in the Years

	1859.	1860.	1861.	1862.	1863.
N. Y. Canals,	3,781,684	4,650,214	4,507,635	5,598,785	5,557,692
Erie Railway,	869,073	1,139,554	1,253,418	1,632,955	1,874,635
N. Y. Central,	834,319	1,028,183	1,167,302	1,387,433	1,449,604
Penna. road,	754,364	968,370	1,087,310	1,528,002	1,713,387
	6,239,430	7,786,321	8,015,665	10,197,175	10,595,218

This statement shows that the total amount of merchandise carried on the three great railroads was more than twice as great in 1863 as it was in 1859, and including the vast business of the New York canals, it is but little short of the same proportions. It cannot be denied that this is overwhelming proof that the increase of the country in material wealth has been great and constant since the war began. The increase on each specific article produced for general markets has been similarly great and regular. At Chicago, Milwaukee, Detroit, Toledo, Cleveland, Buffalo and Oswego, the same steady increase in quantities received and shipped is to be observed. The statistics of the business of each of these cities are now regularly published from authentic records, and from these it may be well to extract some of the more striking facts. At Chicago, the first great point from which the produce of the interior moves to Eastern markets, there was forwarded in five years the following quantities of flour and grain:

		Wheat and Flour reduced to Wheat.	Corn.	Oats, Rye, and Barley.	Total Grain. Bushels.
1859	Bush.	10,598,453	4,349,360	1,806,325	16,754,138
1860	"	15,892,857	13,700,113	1,515,289	31,108,759
1861	"	23,855,558	24,372,725	2,253,584	50,481,867
1862	"	22,508,143	29,452,610	4,526,357	56,487,110
1863	"	18,298,232	24,906,934	12,536,373	54,741,639

The increase of wheat is nearly twice, of corn nearly six times, and of the total of grain much more than three times in 1863 over 1859. An unusual season occurred in 1863, reducing all grain crops largely below the average of years, otherwise the ratio of increase from 1859 to 1862 would have been maintained.

Since 1860, Chicago has also sent to Eastern markets immense quantities of the products of animals; fat cattle, hogs, beef, pork, lard, tallow and bacon. The increase in these products far exceeds the ratio of increase in grain:

	Fat Cattle. No.	Fat Hogs. No.	Beef. Bbls.	Pork. Bbls.	Lard. Lbs.	Tallow. Lbs.	Cutmeats and Bacon. Lbs.
1859	32,500	110,246					
1860	92,000	227,164					
1861	115,000	289,094					
1862	107,966	491,135	151,631	193,920	54,505,123	8,095,531	71,944,010
1863	197,341	862,200	137,302	440,152	58,030,728	4,897,983	95,300,815

The quantities of cured and packed meats, lard and tallow, sent from Chicago previous to 1862, were less in proportion than live stock, and were too imperfectly reported for comparison. It is safe to say that the quantities of 1863 were twenty times as great as those of 1859 or 1860 in such products; in fatted cattle and hogs, it appears that they were nearly seven to eight times as great in 1863 as in 1859.

The city of Milwaukee is another point of outward shipment of Western products to Eastern and European markets. Its increase in quantities is even greater, in proportion, than that of Chicago. The following are the quantities of grain leaving the port for Eastern markets in five years:

	Wheat and Flour Reduced to Wheat.	Corn, Oats, Barley and Rye.	Total Grain.
1859	6,146.737	404,159	6,550,896
1860	9,855,323	139,677	9,995,000
1861	16,672,865	37,715	16,710,580
1862	18,472,705	259,684	18,732,389
1863	15,855,250	1,137,085	16,992,335

In grain, the increase in quantity is nearly threefold in the five years, and in provisions and cured meats the increase is to four times the quantities of 1859.

				Exports of Pork, Beef, Lard and Tallow. Lbs.
1859	.	.	.	10,206,400
1860	.	.	.	11,068,000
1861	.	.	.	14,682,103
1862	.	.	.	30,553,668
1863	.	.	.	41,600,553

Green Bay, a shipping point of Wisconsin, not included in the account at Milwaukee, sent to Eastern markets the following quantities of flour and grain for four years:

	Wheat, bush.	Flour, bbls.	Total bushels.
1860	169,037	36,199	350,032
1861	126,677	64,400	448,722
1862	304,242	95,332	685,570
1863	586,805	140,397	1,288,790

The increase is here nearly fourfold in 1863 over 1860.

Toledo, Ohio, has become a representative point in the receipt and forwarding of interior produce to markets. Its business increased greatly from 1859 to 1863, though not through the construction of new roads, or the opening of new districts.

Quantities sent from Toledo to Eastern markets.

	Flour, Bbls.	Wheat, Bush.	Corn, Bush.	Pork, Bbls.	Fat Cattle, Hogs & Sheep, No.
1860	803,700	5,033,335	5,299,026	not given.	209,608
1861	1,372,111	6,286,936	5,074,366	142,919	281,495
1862	1,585,325	9,827,629	3,813,709	173,328	481,804

Beef, lard, hides, domestic spirits, and many other articles, exhibit a great increase. Domestic spirits reached 160,000 barrels each in 1861 and 1862; beef, 73,480 barrels in 1862; and hides, 6,450,000 pounds in 1862; all forwarded to other and Eastern markets for consumption.

The city of Buffalo is a conspicuously important point at which to measure the quantities of the various staple products of the Northern States. The following is a comparison of the receipts of flour and grain at Buffalo for four years:

	1860.	1861.	1862.	1863.
Flour, bbls.,	1,112,335	2,159,591	2,846,022	2,978,089
Wheat, bush.,	18,502,649	27,105,219	30,435,831	21,240,348
Corn, bush.,	11,386,217	21,024,657	24,288,627	20,096,952
Oats, bush.,	1,209,594	1,797,905	2,624,932	7,322,187
Barley, bush.,	262,158	313,757	423,124	641,449
Peas, bush.,	80,346	83,344	78,266	131,820
Rye, bush.,	80,822	337,764	791,564	422,309
Total bush.,	31,521,786	50,662,646	58,642,344	49,845,065
Flour red'ced to Wheat,	5,561,675	10,797,955	14,230,110	14,890,445
Total in grain, bush.,	37,089,461	61,460,601	72,872,454	64,735,510

This is exclusive of the receipts by the Lake Shore and Niagara Falls Railroads, which are estimated to be 600,000 bbls. of flour, and 300,000 bushels of grain for each of the last two or three years.

The receipt of other products is more difficult to state. Of fat cattle, hogs and sheep, the number received at Buffalo compares as follows for four years :

	Cattle.	Hogs.	Sheep.	Total.
1860,	150,972	145,354	85,770	382,096
1861,	141,629	238,952	101,679	482,260
1862,	129,433	524,916	105,671	760,020
1863,	154,789	474,849	91,128	720,766

Other products received at Buffalo compare as follows, and continue to display the extreme rapidity of increase apparent in all previous cases :

	Pork, bbls.	Beef, bbls.	Bacon, lbs.	Lard, lbs.	Spirits, bbls.
1859,	76,519	81,875	6,953,000	5,379,150	16,211
1860,	16,330	37,522	1,651,600	1,618,303	49,204
1861,	46,363	52,187	2,347,825	3,941,998	111,372
1862,	171,552	123,301	25,687,657	22,471,204	113,253
1863,	303,584	151,605	28,541,150	29,849,939	120,900

Converting the pork and beef to pounds, at 200 lbs. to the barrel, the total weight of meats compares as follows :

1859,	.	.	.	44,010,950 lbs.
1860,	.	.	.	14.040,303 "
1861,	.	.	.	25,999,823 "
1862,	.	.	.	107,129,461 "
1863,	.	.	.	149,428,894 "

The increase in quantity of cured meats is thus ten-fold in 1863 over 1860 at this central point, Buffalo.

There are other points at the eastern extremity of the Lakes at which this great movement of produce may be measured in part ; the chief of which are Cleveland, Erie, Dunkirk, Niagara, Oswego, Ogdensburg and Champlain. But as they all present similar results to those shown at Buffalo, it is not important to cite them in detail. Their general importance is shown in the summary of receipts at the western terminal points of the chief railroads and canals by which the transportation is continued to the seaboard. These points are the western terminus of the Baltimore and Ohio Road ; of the Pennsylvania Central Road, Dunkirk, Buffalo, Niagara, Oswego, Cape Vincent, Ogdensburg, Montreal and Rochester. The sum of receipts at all these points for transportation further eastward was in flour and grain, as follows:

	Flour, bbls.	Wheat, bush.	Corn, bush.	Other grains, bush.	Total in bushels.
1859,	3,760,274	16,865,708	4,423,096	5,264,051	44,354,225
1860,	4,106,057	32,334,391	18,075,778	7,712,032	78,652,486
1861,	6,533,869	46,384,144	29,524,628	10,656,116	119,264,233
1862,	8,433,037	51,220,529	32,998,049	11,286,109	137,669,872
1863,	7,782,920	36,513,952	24,955,885	15,983,111	116,367,548

It should be borne in mind that this is grain and its products alone, and that the year 1863 furnished an unusually small crop for exportation. The staples of meats and provisions more than made up for the relative deficiency in grain in 1863, as compared with 1862.

The Fleet of Lake Transport Steamers.

The movement of quantities of produce so great, called for the building of an immense fleet of vessels, sailing and steam, in 1861, 1862 and 1863. In the fiscal years ending June 30, each, the following numbers of vessels were built on the Lakes:

	Sail vessels.	Steamers.	Total No.	Total Tonnage, Tons.
1860–61,	62	20	82	20,795
1861–62,	60	30	90	35,735
1862–63,	57	24	81	32,348

The active transportation business is, however, best shown by citing the steam-propeller lines existing in 1863 and 1864. These steam-propellers in 1861 and 1862 began to monopolize the carrying trade, which was previously mainly conducted by sailing vessels. At the opening of 1864, Buffalo had four great lines of propellers, viz. :

The Buffalo and Chicago line, ...	6	steamers.
The Western Transportation Company's line, .	12	"
The New York and Erie Railway Co.'s line, .	12	"
The New York Central Railroad's line, .	30	"
Total	32	

In the Western Lakes there were, in addition, five propeller lines connecting with Detroit, Oswego, Montreal and Canadian ports:

The Northern Transportation Company's line, .	8	steamers.
The Grand Trunk line, ...	8	"
The Great Western Railway's line, . . .	7	"
The Detroit and Milwaukee line, . . .	4	"
The Montreal Propellor line, ...	5	"
Total, ...	32	

At Chicago and Milwaukee there were entered and cleared, of different vessels, in 1863:

At Chicago.		At Milwaukee.	
Schooners, ...	447	Schooners, ...	405
Brigs, ...	49	Brigs, ...	20
Barks, ...	92	Barks, ...	70
Propellors, ...	69	Propellors, ...	68
Steamers, large, . . .	5	Steamers, ...	8
Total vessels, .	662		571
Total tonnage, 223,970 tons.		157,852 tons.	

Nearly one-half this immense fleet is new since 1859, and its transportation capacity is nearly twice as great as in 1860, in consequence of the greater tonnage of the steam-propellers recently built.

The same steady increase in quantities may be cited at every point where the productions of the country may be measured. The mines of Lake Superior yielded 65,679 tons of iron ore in 1859, and 280,000 tons in 1863. Of metallic copper the yield was 6,041 tons in 1859 and 10,000 tons in 1863.

Of petroleum, no appreciable quantity existed in 1859, and very little was produced in 1860. The quantities produced and exported for five years were approximately as follows:

Petroleum produced in	1859,	750 bbls. of 40 gallons.		
"	"	1860,	50,000 "	"	"
"	"	1861,	550,000 "	"	"
"	"	1862,	2,000,000 "	"	"
"	"	1863,	2,220,000 "	"	"

The exports cannot be stated definitely for 1861, in consequence of the coal oil then in use; but for 1862, 1863 and 1864, they reached the following quantities and values:

Exports of 1862, 10,834,515 gallons; value $3,183,917
      "   1863, 27,934,044   "   "   10,664,379
"6 mos. 1864, 12,705,698   "   "   6,017,707

In 1864 a much greater proportion of that exported was refined than in 1863.

Iron and Coal.

The quantity of anthracite iron produced in Pennsylvania was nearly as follows for five years:

1859	. . .	286,332 tons.
1860	. . .	313,000 "
1861	. . .	310,000 "
1862	. . .	381,448 "
1863	. . .	430,000 "

The production of charcoal and soft coal iron was nearly four times as great in the loyal States in 1863 as in 1859 or 1860, but the data for a statement are not accessible. In 1858 and 1859, this branch of production had greatly fallen off, and was temporarily suspended, while in 1863 it was active in every locality capable of producing iron.

The coal of the anthracite and semi-anthracite districts of Pennsylvania produced in 1859 was 7,992,632 tons; in 1863 it was 10,226,124 tons. The coal of Maryland was 300,000 tons less in 1863 than in 1859 or 1860; but the soft bituminous coals of Western Pennsylvania, Ohio, Illinois and Iowa, were produced in quantities nearly double those of four years since. The production of lumber, though naturally limited by two causes—the exhaustion of forests and the high price to consumers—shows an increase in 1863 over any former year.

At Chicago and Milwaukee there were received in 1860 292,618,626 feet, and in 1863 443,459,932 feet; an excess in 1863 of more than 150,000,000 of feet. At Albany there was a deficiency of 57,000,000 of feet in 1863 as compared with 1860, but still an increase of 60,000,000 of feet over 1861, with a large increase of timber over both 1860 and 1861. The estimated increase of the lumber product of the Susquehanna region of Pennsylvania was one-fourth upon a total product of 160,000,000 of feet, with a still larger proportion of shipping and other timber.

It may appear superfluous to continue the citation of proofs of the increase of the United States in material wealth for the last five years, yet the point is vital to all the grave questions of resources and finance which we have to meet; and as no cavil can be effective when the absolute quantities are shown to be vastly larger than ever before, we trust our readers will have patience a little farther.

Cincinnati is an inland city, usually thought to be greatly dependent on its connection with New Orleans, and with the planting States generally, for the larger share of its trade. Its receipt of staple products for five years compare as follows:

	Hogs, No. Packed.	Pork, Lbs. Packed.	Tobacco, Hhds. Received.	Pig Iron, Tons Received.
1859	382,826	76,565,200	15,861	33,960
1860	434,499	82,220,311	15,726	37,550
1861	433,799	95,869,579	21,524	23,632
1862	474,467	106,755,000	40,437	28,762
1863	608.457	123,516,771	39,805	39,151

	Flour, Bbls. Received.	Wheat, Bush. Received.	Corn, Bush. Received.	Oats, Bush. Received.	Lard Oil, Bbls. Expor'd
1859	558,173	1,274,685	1,139,022	557,701	41,146
1860	517,229	1,057,118	1,346,208	894,515	50,846
1861	490,619	1,129,007	1,340,690	838,451	53,803
1862	588,245	2,174,924	1,708,292	1,338,950	58,465
1863	619,710	1,741,491	1,504,430	1,312,000	78,429

Every person is aware that the trade of the Mississippi river has nearly ceased since the war began, and a decline of business at Cincinnati would naturally be expected, rather than an increase such as this.

These are a few citations of the quantities of interior produce, entering an interior market—a market from which, in addition to causes of decline before given, the great increase of business in the Lake region may be supposed to have withdrawn a considerable proportion of the trade formerly directed there. The general result, however, is an increase in all the quantities handled, averaging more than thirty per cent. over the quantities of 1860, and in some leading articles, over fifty per cent. of those quantities.

Quantities Exported.

The above may suffice to prove the universal and great increase in the loyal States of the simple quantities of staple articles of production. Every city and every market exhibits the same proportional increase in the quantities produced, handled or sold for consumption. It can no longer be open to doubt, that if staple articles, demanded alike for export and for consumption, constitute wealth, the loyal States were actually far more wealthy in 1862 and 1863 than they were in 1859 and 1860.

Pork, butter, cheese, beef, tallow, tobacco, petroleum, and other articles, exhibit the same extraordinary proportions of increase, both in quantity and value. Perhaps the most direct mode of presenting the point deemed essential in this illustration is to compare the quantities of certain leading exports in 1859-60 with those of 1862-3, or to give the excess in the last named year.

Excess of quantities Exported in 1862-3 over 1859-60.

Wheat, ...	32,005,261	bushels.
Wheat Flour, ...	1,778,459	barrels.
Indian Corn, ...	12,805,321	bushels.
Indian Meal, ...	24,239	barrels.
Pork, ... :	122,878	"
Lard, ...	115,047,077	pounds.
Hams and Bacon, . .	192,399,000	"
Butter, ...	27,531,501	"
Cheese, ...	26,529,255	"
Tallow, ...	48,523,219	"
Lard and Whale Oil, . .	2,013,551	gallons.
Petroleum, ...	27,934,944	" (Calendar year 1863.)
Candles and Soap, . . .	4,041,197	pounds.
Spirits, ...	3,298,195	gallons.
Clover Seed, ...	16,378,800	pounds.
Hops, ...	8,590,824	"

Total excess of grain and flour, in *bushels*, 53,824,072.

Total excess of meats and like animal products, *pounds*, 458,791,659.

Total excess of oils, *gallons*, 29,948,495.

Total excess of spirits, *gallons*, 3,298,195.

Approximate tonnage in excess, 3,845,267,293 pounds; equal to 1,716,766 tons (of 2,240 pounds).

The importance of this increase is most strikingly shown by comparing the quantities of these articles exported in 1859-60 with the increase :

Total weight of these exports in 1859-60, 1,246,388,944 pounds, or 556,423 tons.

Total weight of these exports in 1862-63, 5,091,655,936 pounds, or 2,273,060 tons.

Increase, 3,845,267,293 pounds, or 106,100,461 pounds more than three times the entire export of these articles in 1859-60.

The values of various other articles, as beef, sugar, tobacco, iron, &c., are greater in 1863, while the quantities are less by small differences. Cotton, rice and naval stores, alone, show a marked and large loss of quantities in the exports.

In all this calculation, attention has exclusively been given to the quantities produced and exported, and it reaches the remarkable result, that the absolute tonnage of increase in Northern products exceeds the actual tonnage of Southern products lost to the exports through the rebellion. In weights and quantities that enormous deficiency has already been filled from the surplus products of the loyal States. But we have a right also to claim that almost the entire advance in value from 1860 to the close of June, 1863, was a legitimate and reasonable increase, caused by no inflation or depreciation of the currency, but due solely to the ordinary causes which advance prices—to activity in business and other natural consequences of an almost world-wide demand. The values are justly the profits and wealth of the country to the full measure of their record in the official statements of exports.

An exact comparison of the values of exports of United States produce from the loyal States from 1860 to 1863 is not practicable, but by excluding the trade of ports subsequently closed by the rebellion from the account of 1860 and 1861, a close approximation to the true account will be obtained. A share of Northern products was always exported at New Orleans, and, to a small extent, at other Southern ports; but a share of the staples of the States now in rebellion was also sent to foreign markets through Northern ports. Simply separating the exports at ports subsequently closed from the returns of exports for 1860 and 1861, the increased surplus of the loyal States is as follows·

Domestic Exports of Loyal States.

In 1859-60,	$173,759,664				
In 1860-61,	201,651,554	Increase over	1860,	$27,891,890
In 1861-62,	213,069,519	"	"	"	39,309,855
In 1862-63,	305,884,998	"	"	"	132,125,334

The increase is 76 per cent. in 1863 upon the exports of 1860, and the total value reached is but little short of the value of the exports when cotton, rice and naval stores made up nearly $200,000,000 in value of the total. These three articles were exported in 1859-60 to the value of $196,343,596 in a total of $373,789,274, then the largest to which the domestic exports of the United States had ever attained.

Not to encumber the two points developed in this paper with any detail not absolutely necessary, the case is closed here. Much more might be said, and many facts scarcely less striking may be cited, but it is proposed only to bring out the two great results:—First, that the exchanges of the loyal United States with all foreign nations still produce large annual balances in our favor; and second, that the production of these loyal States has increased almost five-fold at a time when half-hearted friends and open enemies have joined in predicting its ruin.

WASHINGTON, *August 30th*, 1864.

SUPPLEMENT.

The preceding statements and calculations extend no further than to June 30th, 1863, the end of the fiscal year 1862-3 ; and it may reasonably be doubted whether statements not embracing the time since elapsed can fully meet the question as to the strength of the United States to sustain all the trials of the war. At the time they were prepared the accounts for the fiscal year next following, ending June 30th, 1864, were not available in consequence of delay in reporting the imports at the principal ports, and the first publication of the export and import statements for that year was in the Finance Report, prepared December 1st, 1864, and recently issued. The commerce of that year may now be fully stated; and, in addition, the very important commerce of the six months next following, constituting the last half of the calendar year 1864 ;—in all, a year and a half more of the commercial record of the country than was embodied in the previous pages.

This most important and critical additional period fully suffices to make up the entire account of the commercial exchanges during the period of the war, and of the resources developed in a manner so extraordinary during this period. The time is appropriate to state the leading facts and results disclosed, and it is proposed to do so in the manner adopted for previous years, or by citing, first, the summary of foreign exchanges, and then stating the production and movement of leading staples.

At the outset it is necessary to supply one or two defects in the statistics previously given, resulting from imperfect returns at the port of San Francisco. An important omission to return the shipments of gold from that port to London, made on account of, and as the complete property of holders residing in

(41)

the Atlantic cities of the United States, began before the close of the fiscal year ending June 30th, 1862, but the amount in that year was not large.* In the next year, however, the sum of $25,348,690 in gold and silver was so exported; which sum it is requisite to add to the total of exports for that year previously given, increasing the balance in favor of the United States to $104,970,562. From this sum, however, an abatement must be made for difference of values between the exports and imports as reported, which difference will be subsequently stated.

It is also essential to a just consideration of the subject for the entire period, to again call especial attention to the deficiency of the export statement in articles the produce of the United States, arising from the absence of any system of export inspection. No questions of revenue having been connected with the export record until the very recent admission of drawbacks on manufactures of taxed articles, a habit of imperfect preparation of the papers has prevailed, under which, not only were many shipments never cleared at the custom house, but still more of special or single clearances failed to be embraced in the papers finally handed in for record when the ship's clearance was obtained. An officer of the New York custom house, thoroughly conversant with the facts, states that, "It is a startling fact that one-fourth, and I should not be "surprised if it were one-third, of the whole amount of mer- "chandise exported at this port never is reported, and never "will be under the present laws." Many proofs of the extent of this omission have, at various times, been obtained; among them the fact that the Steamship Great Eastern, in June, 1863, actually carried nearly half a million of dollars worth of cargo more than was originally recorded with the ship's clearance at the time of departure. These omissions are not fraudulent, or in intentional violation of the law. They arise from the circumstances inevitably attending the rush of exportation in such vast quantities as have marked the business of the past three years, and the mode of clearance without inspection now admitted. Clearance for both ship and cargo is obtained on

---

* The precise sum was $4,449,431—the correction obtained only in March, 1865.

the mere oath of shipper, clerk, broker or master without any system of inspection, or any possible verification of invoices. It has before been assumed that this deficiency of the export statement is fully twenty per cent. of the total exports, and it more than makes up for all possible deficiencies in the import account. It is sometimes stated that the profits on imports are properly to be considered in adjusting the account of foreign trade; but, if this be true, the deficiency of the export account fully provides for any values properly belonging to the import totals beyond the sums reported on the admission of foreign merchandise to entry. If nothing is estimated for the deficient exports, there can be no claim preferred that the values require correction when finally compared in our own markets.

In the following tabular statements, the last fiscal year previously stated will be repeated, in order to introduce the correction before alluded to in the gold exports of California. For years previous the reader is referred to the preceding pages.

The following is the statement of the total values of exports and imports for two and a half years:

	Total Exports.	Total Imports.	Excess of Exports.
Fiscal year 1862–3	$357,192,936	$252,187,587	$105,005,349
" " 1863–4	339,580,350	328,514,559	11,065,791
Half year, to Dec. 31, 1864,	226,338,148	118,709,293	117,628,855

The most striking fact apparent from these further returns, is the excess of imports in the first half of the calendar year 1864, and the excess of exports in the last half of the same year. These two divisions of the year were really the complement of each other, and corresponding parts of one period, in consequence of the course of trade induced by the increase of the tariff on July 1st, 1864. It was, for some months previous, well understood that a considerable increase in the rates of duty would probably take place at that time; and orders were sent abroad with that expectation from the last months of 1863 until the additional duties of the Act of April 30th, were imposed. An attempt was made to provide for almost the entire requirement of the year following, and this excess of orders and imports was but partially arrested by the addition of fifty per cent. to the existing rates of duty made at the close of April.

After July 1st, the current of foreign trade was almost precisely reversed, and not only were the total values of imports but little more than half the exports, but at least one-half the goods that came in went into warehouse, and were not entered for consumption. An important fact also is to be observed at this time in the large accumulation in warehouse of the imports of the previous six months. Of these imports $38,412,944 in value remained in warehouse on July 1st, a sum properly to be deducted from the total value of imports for that year above given, and making the true balance in favor of the United States on the trade of that year $49,478,-735, instead of $11,065,791.

The unprecedented enlargement of this export trade, after July 1st, is best shown by citing the weekly values going out at New York, which are of produce and manufactures only, not including specie.

Exports at New York for the week ending

July 4th	$5,224,707	Aug. 1st	8,236,012
" 11th	4,394,498	" 8th	6.463,846
" 18th	7,879,920	" 15th	6,808,167
" 25th	8,040,364		

The exports at this and all other ports were, in fact, somewhat more than twice the value of the imports; and of the totals above given, the exports in gold values—which were bullion and specie, and foreign merchandize re-exported—meet more than half the imports.

Gold and Silver exported	$40,105,037
Foreign Merchandize re-exported	20,918,008
Total in Gold values	61,023,045

The sum remaining to be corrected for difference of valuation is $165,315,103. During this period the nominal premium on gold was extravagant, and far beyond the actual differences entering to business. It is assumed that 130 per cent. was fully the business rate, and that, therefore, a deduction at 65 per cent. on the principles before explained, would represent the true value of the exports. At this rate they become, when corrected, $100,190,990, and the total export value $161,214,035.

In a paper too much extended for repetition here,* the fullest practicable analysis has been made of the difference of currencies between the import and export records for the two years during which the premium on gold prevailed—the fiscal years 1862-3 and 1863-4—in the purpose of securing a comparison of intrinsic values, or one in which the terms of the statement should be of equal value. Adding to the sums there given, the amount of specie exportation from San Francisco omitted from the first of ˈthese years, the comparison for the four full years (fiscal) and the half year to the close of 1864, is as follows, all being in gold values:

Fiscal Year.	Exports.	Imports.	Excess of Exports.
1860-61	$410,856,818	$352,075,535	$58,781,283
1861-62	234,388,406	205,819,823	28,568,583
1862-63	318,589,977	252,187,587	66,402,390
1863-64	288,874,101	328,514,559	(Excess of Imports. 39,640,458)
1864, six months	161,214,035	118,709,293	42,504,742

The annual average excess of exports in gold values is thus $28,527,950 for the four fiscal years; and including the half year to the close of 1864, the average becomes $34,803,610, the calculation being for full years. In the two years of high gold premium, the export values, as recorded, were converted to their equivalent in gold by assuming that one-half the amount of premium was represented in the price of these staples, as recorded when exported. The actual corrections made on the produce exports of 1862-3 were at 11½ per cent. for the first six months, and 26 per cent. for the second six months, together reducing the total exports for that year by the sum of $38,568,172. In the next year, 1863-4, the reductions were made quarterly, at 15½, 25, 30, and 44 per cent.,

* North American Review for January, 1865, Art. VI.

respectively, for the several quarters, making a reduction of $50,706,249 from the account for the year. The reduction for the last half year to December 31, 1864, is $65,124,113 and the total for three and a half years, is $154,398,534, taken from the exports on account of difference of valuations. These reductions of course do not apply to the entire mass of exports, since the re-export of foreign goods is always in gold values, and the export of specie and bullion needs no reduction.

A further mention of the warehouse account should be made here. It has been stated that imports to the value of $38,412,944 remained in warehouse on July 1st, 1854. which sum should be deducted from the total of imports for the fiscal year then closing. During the six months following, to December 31st, the proportion going into warehouse greatly increased. At New York, the proportions entered for consumption and for warehouse were

	Entered for Consumption.	Warehoused.
Quarter ending Sept. 30th, 1864,	$20,486,540	$30,650,681
" " Dec. 31st, 1864,	14,878,678	13,744,322
Totals, 6 mos.,	$35,365,218	$44,395,003

Thus nine millions more than half the total imports at New York went into warehouse, and though the returns are yet incomplete, it is evident that the increase in warehouse on January 1st, 1865, is fully ten millions over the amount July 1st, 1864; making a total of forty-eight millions to be deducted from the sum of import values requiring to be met by the exports previous to January 1st, 1865.

In fact the exports, as has been stated, in all cases during the last three years, have precedence in time over the imports; they command the market, and control the exchanges, instead of following upon the imports, and being forced out to pay debts already accrued. For this reason they have paid and continue to pay great profits to all concerned in foreign trade. The values remitted through them, and the exchange drawn against them, are always pressing on the market for sale, and as reckoned in gold values, exchange has almost constantly been below the par. The following table* shows the rates of foreign exchange at New York, for so much of the year 1864 as quotations in gold could be obtained. The class quoted is best banker's sixty day bills, short sight being one per cent. higher, and commercial bills one per cent. lower, on an average. The par is 109½ nearly, calculated at the mint price of the sovereign, which is now $4,86.34.

May 30, 1864	109 @ 109½	Sept. 22 to 26, 1864	108½ @ 109¼
June 21, 1864	110	Sept. 27 to 29, 1864	108½ @ 109⅛
July 25, 1864	109¼	October 3, 1864	108 @ 108¾
August 2, 1864	109	October 4 to 6, 1864	108½ @ 109
August 6 to 13, 1864	108 @ 108½	October 10 to 11, 1864	108 @ 108½
August 15, 1864	108 @ 108¾	October 12, 1864	108 @ 109
August 16 to 19, 1864	108 @ 108½	October 13 to 18, 1864	108½ @ 109½
August 24, 1864	108 @ 108¼	October 20 to 23, 1864	109 @ 208½
August 27 to 31, 1864	108 @ 108¾	October 25 to 28, 1864	109¼ @ 109½
Sept. 3, 1864	109 @ 109⅛	Oct. 31 to Nov. 6, 1864	109¼ @ 109¾
Sept. 5 to 10, 1864	108½ @ 109¼	November 8 to 12, 1864	109½ @ 110
Sept. 12 to 15, 1864	108¾ @ 109½	November 15, 1864	109 @ 109½
Sept. 16 to 21, 1864	109 @ 109½	December, 1864	109½ @ 109¾

In August, and again in October, the market is quoted as enabling gold to be imported from Europe at a profit. In February, 1865, now passing, a still greater decline of exchange has occurred, and gold may be imported at a profit. These conditions would be impossible if, as is too generally believed, the foreign trade of the country had caused a large balance against us and gold was required to be remitted in great amount to pay those balances.

A point which has been thought of vital importance, is the effect of the movement of gold to foreign countries on the stocks held in the United States—the question whether this movement has exhausted the country to an injurious degree. On a previous page, a tabular statement of the exports and imports of gold, and of coin in all forms, has been given, to which it is now necessary to add the sums before alluded to as having been omitted in the return of exports at San Francisco. These sums were, for 1861–2, $4,449,431, and for 1862–3,

---

* See for further statements of interest rates, and the movement of gold in the United States and in Europe, pages 180 to 191, Finance Report, 1864.

$7,140,811, in addition to the corrections before made. The totals for the last three years are :—

	Imports.	Exports.	Excess of Exports.
1861-2,	16,415,052	41,336,3?7	24,921,335
1862-3,	9,555,648	89,505,293	79,949,645
1863-4,	13,155,706	105,125,750	91,970,044

This excess going out in the last two years is simply a diversion of large sums from their usual course when leaving Sàn Francisco—the gold being taken to London from the Isthmus and not to New York. But including all this movement, the result is a gain of gold to the United States since the war, and a diminished average annual shipment abroad. In the six years first given, (on p. 15,) the annual average sent abroad beyond the amounts imported, is $49,945,495; while for the next four years the average is but $45,073,148. The average difference is $4,872,347, and if the supply of gold has not diminised, the gain in the four years would be $25,000,000 nearly. There is reason to believe that the supply from the mines has increased. The lowest admitted annual product is fifty-five millions. At San Francisco the receipts from the mines were :—

In 1861,	41,688,977	1864,	53,512,783
" 1862,	47,471,373	Total,	192.976,487
" 1863,	50,303,349	Average,	48,244,122

At the eastern interior mines the total product of the four years is estimated at $16,500,000, which increases the annual average supply to $52,369,122. The nett export being $45,073,148, the annual accumulation is $7,295,974; and the total gained since the war is $29,183,896.

Thus, after admitting all that appears in the nominal movement of the precious metals within the last two years, the amount gained is thirty millions since the war began. Now, the diversion of gold to London has ceased, and it is received regularly at New York from California, as before the war. And it is also apparent, from many evidences, that the American gold held in London has recently, to a great extent, been invested in United States stocks at the very favorable rates prevailing there, and is thus in effect, already returned to the holders here.

Production and Export of Staple Articles.

In the preceding portions of this pamphlet the latest records of the movement of staple products were given that were available at that date, August, 1864. Since that time many additional results have been made public, and without repeating what was there stated, a further account will here be condensed, coming down, whenever practicable, to the close of the year 1864.

The tonnage movement of the great transportation lines has been given (p. 27) for five years, 1859 to 1863 inclusive, showing an increase in the quantities carried eastward from 3,613,361 tons in 1859 to 6,290,424 tons in 1863. The two great railroads of New York and the Pennsylvania Railroad now show the following increase in 1864 over 1863.

Tonnage Eastward.

	1863.	1864.
New York Central, tons	1,044,259	1,557,148
Erie Railway, tons	1,088,109	1,332,954
Pennsylvania (total), tons	1,580,853	1,805,144
Total tons	3,713,221	4,695,246

Increase of tonnage eastward, in 1864, tons............982,025

The increase in the total of tonnage moved is in like proportion. In tonnage westward the Pennsylvania Road alone increased from 684,560 tons in 1863 to 780,235 tons in 1864.

The movement of produce from the great interior markets is but little increased in 1864 over 1863, but as it was then twice as great as in 1859 it is ample proof of the great and permanent development of the material resources of the country.

At Chicago wheat was received in nearly the same quantity in 1864 as in 1863; corn much less, in consequence of loss of the crop by frost; but other grains were in excess.

	Wheat, bus.	Corn, bus.	Oats, Rye, and barleys, bus.	Other Grains and Seeds, bus.
1863...	17,925,336	24,444,147	12,536,373	7,754,656
1864...	16,312,819	12,557,925	15,644,545	8,765,739

The aggregate is 44,515,289 bushels of bread grains, and nearly five millions of bushels less of grains and seeds than in 1863, the whole of which decline is due to the injury to the corn crop of 1863 by frosts. A large diversion of grain, as well as of other produce, was made southward in 1864, greater in quantity than the like movement in 1862 and 1863. Supplies were taken to New Orleans and the Gulf coast in large amounts, and the whole Mississippi Valley was opened to military occupation. The receipts at Cincinnati show some of this increase, though that is only a partial channel, and represents but a small part of this interior trade.

	Wheat, bus.	Wheat Flr., bbls.	Ind. Corn, bus.	Oats, Rye, &c.	Total bus.
1863	1,741,401	619,710	1,504,430	1,787,111	8,131,492
1864	1,650,759	547,983	1,817,646	1,941,097	8,248,817

High wines, or whiskey, and alcohol, the product of the distillation of bread grains, were produced in 1864 far beyond 1863, as follows:

	1863.	1864.	Increase.
At Chicago, bbls.	137,947	142,846	4,899
At Cincinnati, bbls.	160,858	319,068	158,210

The production of beef cattle, hogs, sheep, and all classes of meats and provisions, also represents the grain product in part. At Chicago, shipments of these articles outward for the two years compare as follows:

	Fat Cattle, No.	Fat Hogs, No.	Beef, bbls.	Pork, bbls.	Lard, lbs.	Cut Meats, lbs.
1863	197,341	862,200	137,302	449,152	58,020,738	95,300,815
1864	179,520	701,850	134,437	229,086	39,923,787	88,375,345

These are the shipments eastward from Chicago only, and in provisions as well as in grain a great diversion of supplies southward is remarked in the reports. It is also true that the packing season is later, embracing less of the business of the winter in 1864 than in 1863. The above comparison, it should further be observed, is with a year of very great abundance of provisions, and while a little short of the quantities for 1863 it is greatly above those of 1862, and three-fold greater than those of 1860.

The trade of Cincinnati in the two years ending August 31, 1863 and 1864, is next in significance as to the general production of the country. As an interior city, it represents the power to consume products as well as to prepare them for exportation, and its condition has the highest value as a representative of the general prosperity. A previous table (pages 35 and 36) brings the statistics of trade at Cincinnati down to the year ending Aug. 31, 1863, and the statement here following compares 1863 and 1864, showing the changes of a single year. The account of flour and grain, having just been cited when giving the business of Chicago, is not repeated in the following list of articles.

			1863.	1864.
Receipts of	Beef Cattle,	number,	31,915	39,152
"	Butter,	pounds,	2,299,800	4,662,900
"	Cheese,	pounds,	6,249,800	5,708,350
"	Cotton,	pounds,	23,448,400	32,296,400
"	Clover Seeds,	bushels,	13,552	19,982
"	Coal,	tons,	320,000	639,016
"	Hay,	tons,	90,908	110,946
"	Hides,	number,	150,501	233,177
"	Iron, pig,	tons,	39,151	44,098
"	" other,	tons,	16,747	28,191
"	" "	pieces,	146,446	181,791
"	" "	bundles,	23,130	46,488
"	Oil, petroleum,	barrels,	20,000	49,031
"	" linseed,	barrels,	34,784	45,107
"	Tobacco,	hogsheads,	33,261	53,769
"	"	bales,	6,981	14,669
"	"	boxes,	31,683	50,063
"	Whiskey,	barrels,	160,858	319,068
"	Wool,	bales,	8,130	14,005
Shipments of	Beef,	barrels,	——	17,548
"	Beer,	barrels,	26,063	31,308
"	Candles and Soap,	boxes,	339,917	280,490
"	Oil, linseed,	barrels,	3,184	11,158
"	" lard,	barrels,	78,429	83,740
"	Leather,	bundles,	28,024	40,385
"	Pork,	barrels,	204,462	183,450
"	"	pounds,	3,580,331	2,721,425
"	Pork and Bacon,	hogsheads,	27,746	34,759
"	Lard,	pounds,	30,514,350	17,218,600
"	Tobacco,	hogsheads,	29,436	48,277

		1863.	1864.
Shipments of Tobacco,	bales,	6,492	22,263
" "	boxes and kegs,	65,457	82,081
" Whiskey,	barrels,	162,007	210,410
" Wool,	bales,	9,790	12,913

The chief increase of quantities is in tobacco, cotton, whiskey, coal, iron and oils; but all articles have increased more or less, when the entire business in them is considered. The values assigned to the receipts and exports at Cincinnati in the commercial reports, give the following aggregates, comparing 1863 with 1864:

	Value of Receipts.	Value of Exports.
1863,	$144,189,213	$102,397,171
1864,	389,790,537	239,079,825

Though these values represent greatly 'increased prices in 1864, as compared with previous years, they establish the fact that an immense growth of general business occurred in both the years named beyond the conditions existing in former years.

The statistics for other great interior markets and distributing points for agricultural staples, are not yet accessible for the year 1864; but they may be estimated generally by what is above given for Chicago and Cincinnati, and by the general increase of tonnage on the great railroads.

The absorption of provisions and products of every class along the whole Western as well as Southern line of the States, beyond the Alleghanies, is another element to be considered in this calculation. Military supplies in large amounts have been required, and a steady increasing emigration has moved westward across the plains to the mining districts of the interior. Much of the produce of Iowa, Minnesota and Wisconsin has been withdrawn for such uses, and by so much the surplus to go eastward was less. When the increased movement southward from St. Louis, and from Illinois, Indiana and Ohio is added to this westward account, it is obvious that to maintain the volume sent eastward at the high point reached in 1863, would require an increase in the production of the whole west of twenty five per cent. in 1864 over 1863. It is believed that the actual increase in the production of all classes of agricultural staples, including tobacco, and textile materials, is fully twenty per cent. in 1864 over 1863; and is, on an average of all articles, three times the quantity that was produced in the same states in 1860. Tobacco, flax, cotton, wool, hemp, sorghum, fruits and many other articles were produced in unprecedented quantities in 1863 and 1864—always much more in the last named year. And these naturally diverted much agricultural labor from the growing of grain and the production of provisions.

Petroleum, it has been previously stated, scarcely existed as a product of exchangeable value with foreign countries in 1860, while in 1863 the value of $10,664,379 was exported. In 1864 a great increase was obtained over 1863, the production having reached 2,500,000 barrels, at least, and the export compared with 1863, was as follows:

Exports of 1863, 27,934,944 gallons; value, $10,664,379
"   1864, 33,467,424   "   "   19,421,752

The export was thus, 836,685 barrels of forty gallons each, of which 455,000 barrels were refined, representing 650,000 barrels of crude: the whole being equivalent to 1,035,000 barrels of crude oil. The consumption of the country was undoubtedly greater than this export, making up the total of production first named. The value of this product when passing into consumption, and when exported, was in the aggregate fully $40,000,000 for the year.

Iron and coal also exhibit a large increase in the quantities produced in 1864 over 1863. The progress of anthracite coal production for the year brought up the total to 10,564,926 tons, an increase of 621,364 tons over the former year. The bituminous coal of Western Pennsylvania is estimated to have produced 3,000,000 tons for the year. Estimating for the consumption of localities at the coal mines throughout the State, it is assumed that the coal raised in Pennsylvania alone reached the aggregate of 15,000,000 tons.

Iron was produced in much greater quantity in 1864 than in 1863, the best estimates placing that of Pennsylvania at 700,000 tons of pig, against 450,000 tons in 1863. No official record of this production exists, however.

Quantities Exported.

Business interests and agencies in the United States were everywhere more active in the period now reviewed, the year and a half ending with 1864, than they were in the previous year; and the consumption of staple articles within the country was enormous. Not only was the demand for the army and navy beyond all precedent, but there was added to this the demand created by extraordinary activity in mining, in manu- factures, in agriculture, and in exchanges among all these inte- rests, of which the central points were the great cities. The supplies required by these interests were almost as much beyond previous example as was the demand for military purposes, and were in direct proportion to the aggregate of business done. The export of the leading staples, before cited, was, therefore, less in proportion to the production than in the two previous years, and in some cases absolutely less, yet it is astonishing to observe that the last half of the year 1864 shows a movement of some articles abroad equal to the whole of either of the previous years. The quantities exported for the fiscal years 1863-4 are also not less than twice as great as in the best year before the war, on an average, as the following comparisons show. It is more significant still of the intrinsic strength and unchecked prosperity of the country that the last half year of this period should maintain so large an export trade, after the outward movement might, for many reasons, be supposed to have passed its maximum point. The following comparison of the quantities and values of the principal articles exported continues the statement with which the first part of this paper closed.

Wheat.			Wheat Flour.		
	Bushels.	Value.		Barrels.	Value.
1859-60,	4,155,153	$ 4,076,704		2,611,596	$15,448,507
1862-63,	36,160,414	46,754,195		4,390,055	28,366,069
1863-64,	23,680,662	31,430,295		3,543,252	25,458,964
Half year, 1864,	6,555,096	13,759,851		1,681,648	16,694,281

Indian Corn.			Indian Meal.		
	Bushels.	Value.		Barrels.	Value.
1859-60,	3,414,155	$ 2,399,808		233,709	$ 912,705
1862-63,	16,119,476	10,592,704		257,948	1,013,272
1863-64,	4,076,789	3,321,526		262,347	1,349,688
Half year, 1864,	778,977	1,077,179		30,532	327,898

Pork.			Lard.		
	Barrels.	Value.		Pounds.	Value.
1859-60,	204,743	$ 3,132,313		40,289,519	$ 4,545,831
1862-63,	327,696	4,334,775		155,336,596	15,755,570
1863-64,	317,345	5,520,648		96,292,144	11,295,332
Half year, 1864,	88,808	3,182,813		25,578,780	5,307,374

Hams & Bacon.			Butter.		
	Pounds.	Value.		Pounds.	Value.
1859-60,	25,844,610	$ 2,273,768		7,640,914	$ 1,144,321
1862-63,	218,243,609	18,658,280		35,172,415	6,733,743
1863-64,	110,759,485	12,303,729		20,795,492	6,121,365
Half year, 1864,	17,476,669	3,703,428		10,257,992	4,387,605

Cheese.			Tallow.		
	Pounds.	Value.		Pounds.	Value.
1859-60,	15,515,799	$ 1,565,630		15,269,535	$ 1,598,176
1862-63,	42,045,054	4,216,804		63,792,754	6,738,486
1863-64,	47,733,137	5,634,515		56,015,375	6,191,743
Half year, 1864,	30,455,993	9,033,262		16,519,261	2,851,452

Lard & Whale Oils.			Petroleum.		
	Gallons.	Value.		Gallons.	Value.
1859-60,	2,335,817	$ 2,382,419		(1863.)	
1862-63,	4,349,398	4,362,229		27,934,944	$10,604,379
1863-64,	1,705,827	2,112,257		33,467,424	19,421,752
Half year, 1864,	1,151,076	2,036,290		(1864.)	

Candles & Soap.			Spirits Distilled.		
	Pounds.	Value.		Gallons.	Value.
1859-60,	11,885,820	$ 1,254,933		4,098,730	$ 1,461,488
1862-63,	15,936,017	1,924,888		7,396,925	3,191,851
1863-64,	13,618,962	1,817,007		1,544,857	850,526
Half year, 1864,	6,185,735	1,161,732		154,630	221,092

	Clover Seed.		*Hops.*	
	Bushels.	Value.	Pounds,	Value.
1859-60,	116,574	$ 596,919	273,257	$ 32,866
1862-63,	389,554	2,185,706	8,864,081	1,733,265
1863-64,	42,213	509,795	5,850,805	1,216,965
Half year, 1864	7,413	58,523	1,443,664	506,181

	Tobacco Leaf.		*Tobacco Man'd.*	
	Pounds.	Value.	Pounds.	Value.
1859-60,	173,844,400	$15,900,547	17,697,309	$ 3,372,974
1862-63,	118,750,200	19,752,076	7,025,248	3,384,544
1863-64,	113,205,800	22,826,359	8,556,282	3,591,944
Half year, 1864,	109,198,333	30,037,443	4,736,332	2,530,271

The quantities of tobacco are maintained in an extraordinary degree, in view of the fact that nearly two-thirds of the export of 1860 came from States now in insurrection.

Generally, the production of articles of prime necessity as supplies to the extent here shown, and the export of these vast quantities as the national surplus at such a time, is without parallel or precedent in the history of nations. The list of articles here cited is a small and incomplete one, taking only such as represent the general condition, as was explained in the previous citation of the quantities exported. The army in the field during this period exceeded any army of modern times, and it might be supposed not only to require all the supplies of this character the country could at any time produce, but it would reasonably be anticipated that stores of provisions would be required from other nations. Instead of this requirement, however, the surplus sent abroad rose steadily in magnitude from the beginning of the war forward, and in the closing months of 1864 the excess of the export over the import trade would more nearly imply that all Europe was at war, and that the United States were devoted to the trade in supplies which such wars have heretofore demanded, than that war at home was trying the national resources, diverting the industry of the country, and absorbing all the supplies that the people left to pursue such industry throughout the country could produce.